MW01139593

The Teacup Deer Fawn

by

Jesse Toland

NEWMAN SPRINGS PUBLISHING
320 Broad Street
Red Bank, NJ 07701

First originally published by Newman Springs Publishing 2021

ISBN 978-1-64801-995-1 (Paperback)
ISBN 978-1-64801-996-8 (Hardcover)
ISBN 978-1-64801-997-5 (Digital)

Printed in the United States of America

In loving memory of the most loyal and loving companion
I could have ever asked for,
my teacup deer fawn
Chihuahua, Rosie.

To my mother and father,
Larry and Debbie,
thank you for everything,
I love you.

There in the field they lay, three newborn teacup-sized deer fawn bleating away. As they open their eyes, there they see, a loving mother who will show them the way.

With determined minds and wobbly legs, they take their first stance to seize the day. First, they nurse their first drink, then their mother will say, "It's time," and then they're off and away.

4

Through town, they roam to find a new temporary home. A place to bed down and stay safely tucked away. This way, Mother may go off and graze.

But one of these fawns is special you see, for he is fearless and adventurous unlike his family. Whether it be making new friends or scaling rock walls, this little fawn did it all.

Before too long, Mother had said, "There is where we will go and lay down to bed." As they approached, the siblings stayed close, except for a certain adventurous bloke…

"Look, Mom! Look at me! I'm big and strong, just watch and see!"

Before Mom could speak, the baby fawn slipped and fell off his feet.

The little fawn slid and got wedged between two rocks. His mother tugged and she tugged, but it was no use. As hard as she tried, she couldn't pull him loose.

Mother cried and cried because she knew what she must do. She must go and find a safe place for the other two.

14

The baby, once fearless, now struggled in fear, but did it in vain for no one was near. As the hours went by, the little fawn feared, would he even live to see his first year?

Then out of the blue drove up a machine from which emerged a strange family. This family was strange because they walked on two legs!

Soon, the mommy yelled, "Over here, over here! Look there's a baby deer!"

Then came the father and son shocked by what they would see, a little baby deer who fell off his feet!

Carefully, the daddy pulled and he pulled till the little baby deer pulled free with a moan. They laid him in the grass for his mother to see, but she looked on obliviously.

They waited and waited, but unfortunately, the mother turned and left unknowingly. Now the sky darkens as the rain starts to fall, and the son thought to himself, *I can't do nothing at all!* so he grabbed himself a blanket and returned to the fawn.

Tired and hungry, there lay the fawn, for he was saddened and missing his mom. But the son was not done, so he picked up the fawn and lay him under the window to wait for the sun, and there the poor baby slept and waited till dawn.

The Mommy and Daddy woke in a hurry to make sure the baby would not worry. They swept him up, and off they would go to the back yard to nurture his growth!

They made him a bed of cushion and cloth, then fed him milk from a bottle to soothe his cough. Before too long, the son awoke to find his new friend was strong and afloat.

As the son sat down, the deer rose to his feet and jumped in his lap harmoniously. With a tear in his eye, the son leaned in for a hug, now they are best friends no matter what.

In a moment or two, more and more of this strange family appeared. Shocked by what they would find, a young man and his friend, the four-legged kind.

All day they played, and though the bond was made, the fawn remembered yesterday. So the fawn called out hoping beyond hope, his mother would hear and return for the bloke.

Soon the son's auntie would cheer, "There beyond the fence! It's the mother deer!" then just like that, she disappeared. They waited and waited, then waited some more for his mother and siblings to come for their fourth.

Later that day, there the mother was, waiting for her baby out in the front. The son kissed and he hugged as they said their goodbyes, vowing to see each other again as the days go by.

As the little fawn began walking away, he thought long and hard about his first day. So much had happened, some good and some bad, but none more important than the lesson he'd had. Now a family reunited, a mother and her sons, clip-clopped up the street into the sun.

About the Author

Jesse Toland is a twenty-six-year-old native of a small town in Northern California. At the age of nine, his parents gifted him a Chihuahua puppy with which they had been told was a teacup deer fawn Chihuahua. Shortly after her passing nearly sixteen years later, Jesse and his family returned home one evening to find a newborn deer fawn fighting for its life, thus becoming the inspiration for this book.

CPSIA information can be obtained
at www.ICGtesting.com
Printed in the USA
BVHW061713150721
612042BV00006B/758